Ragamuffin Cats as Pets

Caring For Your Ragamuffin Cats

Ragamuffin Cats facts, care, breeding, nutritional information, tips, and more!

By Lolly Brown

Foreword

"Cats, felines, purr-face, grabby-paws, chatter-box, silent-stalker, and curious-kitty, funny – face." It is clear that we have been bitten by the feline-bug and can't get enough of our cat friends who are surprisingly some of the cleverest animals in the pet-realm. In this book, you will learn all about a cat breed which was produced and got its beginnings in the United States.

Many of the pet cats we see today come from far off places and originate from different countries. The Ragamuffin Cat is one which we can classify as All-American having been developed in the shores of these United States. It is a fairly young breed with it showing up on the feline-map of breed in the 1960s. You are cordially invited to get to know more about this beautiful cat with a laid back personality. Let's have you discover as we reveal what it would take for a potential owner of this lovely feline to purchase (or adopt one), what to look for in terms of cat health and breeder credentials.

Table of Contents

Chapter One: Introduction

This All-American feline, the Ragamuffin, is a variant of the Ragdoll which was established and classified as a separate breed in 1994. It is a domestic cat breed who has been likened to an Angora rabbit because of its lush rabbit-like fur and amiable personality. They are heavy-set feline breed with muscular features. One really awesome feature of the Ragamuffin cats is the time it takes for them to fully mature.

Ragamuffin cats take about four to five years to mature, so just imagine having a kitten-like cat love on you for that amount of time! Generally classified as a substantial-bodied feline, the appearance of a Ragamuffin cat include being physically rectangular-shaped, with shoulders which support a short neck and abroad chested body. It adorable faces sits on a broad head, classified as a modified wedge. It sports a slightly rounded forehead which dips to its nose.

Its rectangular shaped body starts at a broad chest trailing down to broad shoulders. Its hindquarters are slightly heavy muscled and its back legs should be equal to the breadth of its shoulders. Its lower abdomen should sport fatty pads. They come in an assortment of colors and color patterns. Their medium-length coat, which lengthens more in the belly area, is plush, thick, full, supple and silky to the touch. As plush as their coats are and get, it does not mat or clump easily and is quite easy to manage as long as it gets a routine grooming it needs.

The Ragamuffin has a ruffled look to its physical appearance since its fur length is longer around the facial area. Fur length is to be slightly longer at the edges of its face and neck. Its coat increasingly lengthens from the top of its cranium and trails down softly to its shoulder blades all the way to its back. The Ragamuffins coat, on its sides and stomach, is of medium to medium-long length. Its coat is plush, soft and easy to manage with weekly routine grooming.

Ragamuffin cats come in many colors and color patterns; with some sporting white others not. There are some color patterns which are rarer and more in demand than others, but a pure white Ragamuffin is rare and therefore generally more in demand than most.

In the 1960's, a regular, domestic, non-pedigreed, long-haired cat fondly called Josephine who many times previously had given birth to several litters of kittens - all of which appeared like run of the mill, typical kittens - got into an accident and as a result was injured. Josephine was taken to a laboratory at the University of California soon after the road accident and was tended to until she recovered. Caregivers of Josephine noted that after she had recovered the next litter she gave birth to be exceptionally friendly felines. Noticing that the subsequent litters produced after that litter an established cat breeder, Mrs. Anne Baker, acquired several of these amiable kittens from Josephine's humans with the intent of creating what we presently known as the cousin of the Ragamuffin, the original Ragdoll cat.

It was in the mid-1970s when Ann Baker made up her mind to turn her back on the traditional associations and set up her own registry. She first got the name "Ragdoll" trademarked for a new sort of cat which had no relation to the original Ragdolls. Her registry called the International Ragdoll Cat Association (IRCA). The association Ms. Baker had set up imposed very strict standards to those who desired to sell or breed Ragdoll cats under her foundation. One stringent requirement was that Ragdolls registered under IRCA could not be registered with other breed associations.

A select cluster of IRCA member breeders made up their minds to break away and establish their own group due to the progressively strict restrictions on Ragdoll breeding. Because of the trademark on the Ragdoll moniker, the breakaway group had to come up with a different name. Ideas were tossed around and the name Liebling Cats was on the table. However because the people couldn't make up their minds and come to a consensus about this name, they brainstormed more and one member piped in the name Ragamuffin, jokingly pointing out that the cat seemed like a lost waif. It was like a light bulb switching on and everybody loved it. Hence they renamed their IRCA collection of Ragdoll cats, Ragamuffins.

With the aim of improving the genetic health, temperament and personality of the Ragamuffin breed, the group set forth to cross breed the Ragamuffin with domestic long haired cats, Himalayans and Persians. They didn't stop there and allowed a select few to cross-breed with the original Ragdolls. Cross breeding Ragamuffins with Ragdolls ended in 2010 for Ragamuffins recognized by the AFCA. Since then only felines who came from parents with one Ragamuffin parent out-crossed with and accepted feline of the AFCA presently quality to be called a Ragamuffin. The Ragamuffins registered under the Cat Fanciers Association (CFA) are only accepted if both the cats' parents are Ragamuffins.

It was the United Feline Organization (UFO), and the first cat association, which accepted the breed to register under full show and champion status. Other major feline associations continued to refuse acceptance of the Ragamuffin as a recognized sort mainly due to its close relation to the Ragdoll. However the American Cat Fanciers Association (ACFA) did accept the Ragamuffin as a recognized breed. In February of 2003, the Cat Fanciers Association (CFA) finally welcomed Ragamuffins into the Miscellaneous Class and much later, in February of 2011 advanced Ragamuffins to the Championship Class. These cat associations accept Ragamuffins of all colors, however, under CFA standards; Ragamuffins with color points are not acceptable.

Chapter Two: What Are Ragamuffin Cats?

Not to be confused with its close cousin the Ragdoll, the Ragamuffin is now a separate breed of its own. Although little documentation and information is available about how the Ragamuffin was developed, speculations about its occurrence are hinted like it was probably developed by crossbreeding it with some breeds with long hairs like the Birmas, Persians, other long-haired domestic cats and Turkish Angoras.

Interesting Personality Facts and Traits of the Ragamuffin Cat

This densely coated cat is a versatile companion to many and has been said to shadow their humans going about their day around the house. It is very open to join in child's play doing different playtime activities. You will find it willingly allowing itself be dressed up for calendar photo shoots or sitting down to high tea. It has an open and exceptional nature and makes for a good travel buddy during holidays and vacations. The Ragamuffin is not fussy at all and would even be willing to be taught to walk on a leash.

Don't let the lush fur of the Ragamuffin's fool you into believing that it is difficult to groom because it is, in fact, one of the most low maintenance cats owing to their silky soft fur which isn't prone to tangling. That being said, it is highly recommended that you tend to its coat by routinely giving it a good brush once or twice a week to prevent its coat from matting. It enjoys gentle quiet time with its human family and won't have a problem allowing you to give it its weekly grooming routine as long as you are gentle and revere it with kindness.

Just like other felines, the Ragamuffin sheds it fur but not in excess. So even with its dense coating, maintaining your Ragamuffin won't be too much trouble. However, always make sure to ask for the cat's history because it has been noted that Ragamuffins with Persian ancestry are more prone to coat matting.

Apart from the weekly brushing your Ragamuffin needs, the only other grooming requirements it would need would be ear cleaning, nail trimming and at least twice a month tooth brushing. We advise that you use a swab of cotton moistened with an ear cleaning solution approved by your vet. While you're at it get a recommendation about what toothpaste to use to brush your feline's teeth. As healthy a breed the Ragamuffin is it is a feline and most felines are prone to periodontal disease.

The size of the Ragamuffin is often compared to that of a small dog since it can weigh anywhere from 10 to 20 pounds. A large cat with an equally large heart! Keep this utterly friendly feline indoors. Because its docile temperament Ragamuffins have a tendency to warm up quickly to people who show it kindness and could give the wrong ideas to someone who may fancy the feline and, worst case scenario, take it home to make it their own. Keeping the feline indoors will also protect it from road traffic and accidents, diseases carried and spread by feral animals and attacks from wild animals and big dogs who don't like cats. The Ragamuffin cat, if kept and cared for under optimum conditions, can enjoy a life of up to 3 years or more.

The Ragamuffin Cat Breed History

The Ragamuffin is a cousin and descendant of the Ragdoll cats. It is a very young sort of feline, recently given its own classification and breed in 1994. It was Ann Baker, a Persian cat breeder who discovered the litter of kittens in the 1960s, which were birthed by a neighbor's cat who was non-pedigreed. The kittens, Ann realized were a lot more laid back and friendlier than most cats she had come across in the past.

Josephine was the name of the mother of this litter, and Ann was fortunate enough to be allowed to purchase some of these kittens. She then proceeded to breed them and was able to successfully develop a few breeds, which included the Ragdoll. She classified and labeled them all under "Cherubim."

Soon enough other breeders got wind of these new friendlier cats and decided to get in the game and join Ann in raising the descendants of Josephine. Ann frowned upon participating in accredited cat registries but ironically founded a cat registry of her own which she called the International Ragdoll Cat Association or IRCA. She then proceeded to trademark the "Ragdoll" name. Ragdolls are large felines with big, blue eyes and color-points. They don't differ too much from their cousins the Ragamuffins with their medium long coat, and lovely dispositions.

Ms. Baker kept a tight rein on the procedures of breeding Ragdolls and because of the stringent requirements she adhered to and imposed some breeders broke away of the controlling Ann in the 1970s. This group toiled to get major kitten associations recognizes their sweet Ragdoll kittens. Ms. Baker kept leadership and control of the Cherubim kitten breeding when the first group broke away to establish the Ragdoll breed in other associations. There were however a considerable number f people who believed and championed Ann's cause and stayed with the IRCA and continued breeding the Cherubim and Ragdoll cats.

The Beginnings of the Ragamuffins

The 1990's saw Anne age and as she did she had started imposing more demanding requirements of the breeders under the foundation she established. Ultimately a second breakaway group comprised mostly of the breeders who stayed, left to form a group independent of Anne's foundation in 1993. It was this group of breeders who formed the Ragamuffin foundation. A blend of all the Cherubim breeds were the first pool of cats the foundation started out with and they noted how these kittens turned out to be more friendly and lovable with easy-going personalities that seemed to thrive in almost any conducive environment friendly to cats.

The breakaway group from IRCA began establishing their association for Ragamuffins on a difficult note with unregistered felines. They had to build up a standard that was unlike the standards made up the founding breeders of IRCA. It was only during the period of urgency when the submission for the new standards was due and because Ann had trademarked the Ragdoll, the group had come up with a new name through happenstance and jokes. Since the kittens were originally dear little urchins from the street one of the founding breeders jokingly called them Ragamuffins. Not everybody agreed with this name but agreed to it and it is the name that stuck and is known up to this present day.

The Ragamuffin (as the group agreed to spell it) is a small breed having only several breeders in Europe and the United States. Their primary consideration is the protection and promotion of the Ragamuffin kittens health and welfare. This group pays careful mind to the genetics and health care of the kittens. Proper utilization of breeding methods comes in a close second on their list of priorities.

The Ragamuffin Cat Temperament

Ragamuffin felines are lauded for their loving personalities. They practically live on human attention and companionship, and are frequently discovered to be waiting for their humans at the door. Your lap is where they would usually be found, curled up in a cloud of happiness for hours. Ragamuffins are extremely patient with little folk and openly welcome the company of other pets.

They are playful, like to cuddle and are not at all aggressive. They love lap felines who occasionally vocalize when roused from the reverie of your company. Owners of these felines get to enjoy the cat's kitten hood for a long time since it takes at least four to five years from the ragamuffin cat to reach maturity. Be prepared for a playful kitten and cuteness overload!

Chapter Three: Ragamuffin Cats vs. Ragdoll Cats

Recognized as two distinct breeds by the Cat Fanciers Association both the Ragdoll and Ragamuffin cats are big, sweet, and docile cats which can weigh up to a hefty 15 pounds. If you are searching for a cat that is large but friendly, then you have made the right choice of getting to know the ragamuffin. In this chapter, we'll further discuss about the difference between ragamuffin and ragdoll cats as well as their behavior towards other pets and other people.

Coat Quality and Color

Excluding cats with pointed colors, the CFA accepts any pattern and color for the Ragamuffins and this includes white Ragamuffins. Color and pattern is what separates the Ragamuffins from the Ragdoll because the Ragdoll sort is color pointed exclusively. This means that overall color is lighter than the color of the ears, legs, tails, and face, even though the Ragdoll can occasionally sport white paws and legs typically called "boots" and "gloves." The coat of both breeds is described by the CFA to be medium long with full tails. A distinction of the Ragamuffins coat which, compared to the Ragdoll's coat with lesser coat matting characteristics, does not easily mat.

Another significantly distinct difference in the ragdoll and ragamuffin breeds would be their eyes. Standards of the CFA say that both feline breeds have big eyes, however the eyes of the ragamuffin are walnut shaped and rounder in comparison to the oval shaped eyes of the ragdoll. Eye colors also come into play in terms of distinguishing both breeds; Ragamuffins are allowed to have any eye color whilst ragdolls must only have blue eyes.

As family pets, both the ragamuffin and ragdoll breeds are lauded for their affectionate and sweet natures.

Even if the CFA recommends one or the other as companions, the cat association distinguishes the ragamuffin sort to be a better pairing with children mentioning the ragamuffin's patient and calm temperament toward children.

These two breeds were developed with neither of them occurring naturally, however the real history of the ragamuffin breed development is vague and mostly unclear. On the other hand, the Ragdolls are documented to have been produced in California during the 60's by a cat fancier turned breeder, who noticed the distinct endearing traits of the kittens birthed by long-haired, white domestic feline she purchased. She then began breeding the feline she purchased to some of the cats she found or owned and hence the birth of the Ragdoll.

Should You Opt for More Than One Ragamuffin Cat?

Short answer in question form is, why shouldn't you? With its docile demeanor and amiable, laid back personality there is no reason not to get a pair, or more, of ragamuffins. Some individual have 4 to 8 of these furry felines and just can't get enough of them! However, there are a few questions you will have to ask yourself like the following:

- Am I ready to be cuddled up to at random times?
- Do I want to be shadowed and be followed by my cats when I move around the house?
- Since they are so adaptable to almost any situation or environment without being bothered by change would I be willing to take them on vacations?
- Can I afford to take on the financial responsibility of owning two cats?
- Can I TAKE ON the responsibility and work it takes to raise more than one Ragamuffin?
- Will I be able to give all of them the time they need to play and frolic?
- Is my home space sufficient enough to house my family and a litter of Ragamuffins?

Give yourself honest answers to those questions and you should be able to get closer to making a decision. In the meantime, read on as we reveal more about caring for these adorably laid back, fluffy cats.

Does Ragamuffin Cat Get Along Well with Other Pets?

There are dogs that are meant and bred to be hunters, and this goes the same for cats. If you have birds or smaller furry animals in your home, you might want to rethink this. The thing about pets is we really won't be able to tell until we have tried to integrate them into our homes. There are dogs who have been reported to "adopt" little kitten their owners have brought home. Others report that their cats have taken a liking to spending time and sharing company with their pet birds.

You want to make sure that you pair up your pets according to their natural, personality traits. This means you don't want to pair a ratter dog or cat with a hamster or a mouse. That would just spell disaster!

However, you Ragamuffin has such mellow-temperament that it would probably get on with your other pets well as long as they are feline-friendly. The joy of hearing the pitter-patter of little paws is a joy like no other. Ragamuffin cats are famously excellent players and would love nothing more than to keep company and endless playtime with other Ragamuffins. In other words, it is all a matter of patience, observation, watchful supervision, and time.

The Ragamuffin and You

Are you the cuddling type? Then look no further because the Ragamuffin is just the pet you are looking for. There are so many reasons why people are attracted to the ragamuffin breed and those reasons don't end with their remarkably distinct appearance. The Ragamuffin feline, with its great disposition and extreme intelligence, has consistently been a greatly sought after feline favorite because many owners of this cat sort talk about it being perfect as a family companion.

Homes with existing feline-friendly pets and young children have notably welcomed the Ragamuffin with hardly any issues due to its even-temperedness. Families with children get to enjoy family routines which include and involve the feline being raised alongside them. The ragamuffin has been a great addition of inspiration and joy to the countless families who have discovered the rewards of living with one.

They warm up easily to people so be wary that you not let them out of the house without a leash (yes, they can be highly trainable to walk with one) and if given the right amount of space and time they will crawl up to your lap and contentedly curl up there for as long as you allow.

It is a gentle feline who is not at all bothered to be around strangers or be in new places. It can hardly be called shy because once it gets a feel of no impending human danger to it, it will sidle up to you and possibly cuddle. True to its feline nature, the Ragamuffin reserves making judgments about anything or anyone until it has studied, surveyed and observed everything and everyone.

Once the consensus is in and it determines you to be of no threat to itself, the Ragamuffin will have no qualms in letting you feel how valuable you are. These breeds of cats are deeply devoted and openly affectionate to their human families. The Ragamuffin is a sweet companion to all the members of the family and will expressly be glad to welcome you at the door when you return home. This feline sort will be ecstatic to locate a spot on you next to you or in the general space you are occupying, where it can share downtime with and be close to you.

Cats are keenly sensitive toward each of their human family's mood and this feline trait has been discussed to extents amongst feline owner as positive traits of the Ragamuffin. This feline breed will sense the change in the emotions of its human family and would seemingly mirror the caregiver's inner workings. It would even get closer to the distressed individual seemingly offering comfort in periods of worry or distress.

Contrary to popular legend that felines are stubborn and aren't trainable beings, felines are actually quite adept to understanding human commands and instructions given enough time. This is a trait the intelligent yet laid back Ragamuffin possesses. With enough socialization training through repeated human exposure they are able to understand and learn tricks they are taught.

Find a favored toy which it can manage to carry in its tiny jaws, show it to your Ragamuffin and throw it a fair distance. Do it often enough and observe your Ragamuffin fetch the toy. Ragamuffins if given the free rein of the home it will lord over the family. So, if you are the alpha-type, you would want to set rules and boundaries at the onset of the relationship.

The Ragamuffin is a very social cat who has no problems being around new places and people. Generally, cats can get pretty skittish around strange humans and new environments, but not your Ragamuffin cat. It manages to adjust quite well in new situations so it is the perfect companion to take with you on a routine shopping trip or an extended vacation.

Just give it a little time and you will see how easily your Ragamuffin integrates itself to the family with no problems. Anyone who loves to cuddle and be cuddled would be perfect candidates for Ragamuffins. That makes up about all families with little children, older people, the younger set and everyone in between.

Be ready to be shadowed by your Ragamuffin because it is a social cat who likes to get into the mix of what you are doing. It is not as vocal as other felines are and would usually reserve its two-cent worth unless you start speaking to it. As long as it is around you, it is a happy camper.

Ragamuffins are actively playful and can get really excited when at play, just like most felines. Just watching them at play will make your heart melt into mush. Call out to them so they get used to their names and wait for them to look into your eyes and be swept away. The felines create really strong bonds with their humans so it is no wonder that feline aficionados talk about and miss their furry buddies when they are away from home for too long.

It'll take no more than a heartbeat to get your own ragamuffins integrated into the family. Remember though, that if you have young children in the house, training will also need to be given to your little humans on how to respectfully handle felines. Ragamuffins have a penchant for going limp in your hands and arms when picked up and love nothing more than to be cuddled like a baby. Swaddle it up in a blanket as you carry it in your arms and it will purr contently in your presence. Stare into its big, walnut shaped eyes and be transported to a place of utter calm.

The measure of trust it has is readily shared for the people it holds dear. In fact, they are such a trusting sort that it would even eagerly greet guests at the door when they sense company! Ragamuffins are hardly vocal felines. Like most felines they will hardly ever meow at other cats (cats who talk to each other usually yawl). But your feline, when it meows at you is actually trying to communicate with you, so consider yourself lucky when it does. You will in time be able to realize what it is trying to say to you if you allow yourself to comprehend and give it enough time.

Mealtimes are usually a chatty time, especially when your Ragamuffin senses that you are about to feed it. It will hound you, dog you and probably get underfoot. You can "train" your cat to a certain extent. You can't expect it to be as trainable as dogs as cats are by nature pretty independent thinkers. However, with enough chatter, you will notice that your ragamuffin seems to understand your simple commands. Like "let's go!", "come here", "no", "good girl" and respond by head butting your hand, curl up around your feet or plop itself where you are seated.

The Ragamuffin adores when it is given attention and hugs by its owners. It thrives gentle hugs and tender stroking. It enjoys perching by the window and watches the sights of the world outside. It is happiest in the safety and comfort of home and family above all.

Speaking of the outdoors, since Ragamuffins are few, you want to keep your Ragamuffin indoors at all times because of a number of reasons. First, they are an attractive sort and with their friendly nature you might just lose one of them to a stranger if they get picked up by a random person. Second, you want to steer clear of feral animals which may infect it with disease and illness. Third, you want to keep them safe from vicious attacks. Fourth, you want to keep them away from road traffic which may result in dire and heartbreaking consequences. Children and Ragamuffins are the same, they pair up so well and will enjoy years and years of loving interaction. Do remember to teach young children how to properly handle cats so that they cat warm up to little tots too.

Chapter Four: What Does it Cost to Keep a Ragamuffin Cat?

The monthly expenditure of raising your Ragamuffins should be more consistent as the months and years go by. As long as they are kept healthy you won't need to dole out as much as you initially did because you would have already invested in the necessary sundries. Don't get stuck of spending outside of your income because this will later be a source of frustration. You need to get your finances sorted out and figure out the monthly costs raising your Ragamuffins before they even get to you.

Acquisition Costs

Know the going rate of Ragamuffin kittens because this empowers you to evaluate the good offers from the shady ones. Cost of a purchasing a Ragamuffin greatly depends on where you are getting one. If getting from a rescue/adoption facility, there is usually a down payment given to the establishment of anywhere between $200-$300 which is deducted from the total cost of around $1,800. This is a first come-first served deal where the person who makes the down payment is given priority.

When purchasing outright from a breeder, and do look for a reputable one, the cost can be anywhere from between $800 - $4000 USD. These prices may seem high and yes agreeably so because Ragamuffins are few and far between. Breeders of these cats are few. And these prices should be inclusive of all papers, vaccinations, initial medical cost and other related health expenses.

Shipping Costs

You will need to factor in shipping fees into the initial price because this will be a hefty chunk of money depending on the distance it will be coming from. Because ragamuffins are pretty rare, there could be a possibility that you may need to order your ragamuffin kitten outside of your home state. We have included a list of breeders located in different parts of the United States in this book for you to study and get in touch with when you have made your decision.

Shipping costs may vary from $175-$400. To make sure about the amount you need to pay for shipping, get in touch with a company that does this. A reputable out of state breeder would usually have a handling company on its contact list which they trust dealing with, so the amount may be included with the purchase price. Remember to ask all sorts of pertinent questions when you are at this stage of getting your Ragamuffin.

Kitten and Cat Supplies

There are breeders (mostly those who are of good repute) will hand over little extras to you for your kitten, like feeding bowls, toys and other stuff used by you Ragamuffin while under their care. Take into account that if your Ragamuffin is being transported to you from out of state, these sundries could be factored into the shipping costs. Again, ask questions.

These are other things you will have to purchase or put aside money for as you get ready to welcome your Ragamuffin home:

- Vaccination for kittens: $50 - $100
- Vet visit: $35 - $50
- Treats: $5 - $15
- Kitten Food: $15-$30
- Drinking and feeding bowls: Invest in the sturdy sort which are non-toxic and easy to clean - $50 - $150
- Bed and blankets: $25 - $100
- Harness and/or Leash: $5 - $25
- Brush and comb (get one of each): $7 - $50
- Clippers and Trimmers: $6 - $50
- Litter Boxes: $15 - $200
- Kitty Litter: $5 - $35
- Liners and mats: $2 - $40
- Filters and deodorants: $4 - $25
- Waste Disposal: $3 - $30
- Toy Crate: $10 - $150
- Toys: $1 - $50
- Cat carrier: $25 - $200
- Tooth brush $5-$10
- Vet approved toothpaste $10-$15
- Scratching posts $50-$200
- Vet approved pet cologne $20-$30

Below is a short list of what you would expect to spend each month after. This list and the one before that are good for one cat.

Monthly Costs

- Kitten Food: $15-$30
- Treats: $5 - $15
- Kitty Litter: $5 - $35
- Waste Disposal: $3 - $30
- Liners and mats: $2 - $40
- Filters and deodorants: $4 - $25

Expect these prices to differ according to your taste. Prices will also be variably different depending on the place or site you are purchasing from. Best to get these all sorted out early on so that you can start organizing spaces in your home and move around things if needed. Make good investments on the sundries your new Ragamuffins will need as they will be using these for a long time to come. Make sure that you clean them on a regular basis to rid it of fur balls, dust accumulation, and other undesirable matter.

We recommend shallow, stainless steel or porcelain bowls for feeding and eating since cat whiskers get in the way. Slow feeding bowls allow your cat to eat at a pace and not have it scarf down their food too fast. You could also get one of those fancy cat feeders which train your cat to release only a certain amount of food at a time - this helps to prevent overeating as well.

Speaking of food, the quality of food will greatly play a big factor on your cat's health and wellness. Be sure that you choose just a bit of food at the beginning. You want to serve it bits of food at a time so that you can figure out which they prefer. Make sure that the food you choose will give them the optimum balance in nutrition. Not only will balanced nutrition serve them well physically, it will also optimize them mentally.

What Are The Pros and Cons of Owning a Ragamuffin Cat?

There are only a few breeders of Ragamuffins in the United States and across the globe. These breeders, who are members of cat societies and foundations, are bent on the healthy development and welfare of Ragamuffins.

They are dedicated to employing only the most humane breeding methods to grow the Ragamuffin population. Hence, the Ragamuffin is one hardy cat who has very little medical issues. However, they like most other felines (and us humans), are still susceptible to some conditions. But given the right breeding practices, the correct nutritional balance, the love and care they need, they are one of the healthiest felines in the cat world.

They are not as prone to medical issues as other pedigreed felines are, and this makes caring for them a lot simpler than raising another pedigreed breed of cat. As a rule, no matter what pet you decide to raise, the research you do before making a purchase allows you to set reasonable expectations. This period of learning and getting to know their specific needs is vital to a successful pairing between you and pet. Smooth incorporation and transition of your new pet into your home, family and life depend on it.

You will have to ask questions and study up on the specifics of the pet to empower yourself in order to know everything you need to know about your new pet's parental history, the breeding methods employed to develop the pet and possible medical conditions an animal may be prone. Taking in a new pet entails responsibilities for the long haul so it is just right that you ask the breeder and a pet health care provider about possible illnesses your new pet might develop. It will be up to you to find out what to avoid keeping your cat safe and healthy.

All felines can suffer from stress most especially if separated from the mother when they are too young. You have to be in the position and prepared to recognize these symptoms of anxiety in a pet. Anxiety and stress are manifestations of insecurity and fear in the feline. You will notice this when they are skittish even around you, they don't eat which results to a weaker immune system, they hide and stay away from company and so on. To avoid this, make sure that the Ragamuffin you are getting is at least 12 weeks old. It would have been weaned off of its mother and would be more open to exploring on their own away from maternal care.

They are usually vaccinated during this period because they would be old enough and you'd be sure (with breeder guarantee, of course) that you are getting a well taken care of cat, who has been seen by a vet and who would have been introduced to socialization. If your job is the sort which keeps you away from home for long periods of time, you might want to rethink raising a Ragamuffin because it will require your company and companionship. They thrive on being with their loved humans and dote on your attention. However, if there is an equally responsible adult who can mind and keep it company during your absence then there shouldn't be a problem. Ragamuffins are also fairly independent with and able to amuse themselves whilst you are gone. Just make sure that they have enough toys and cat-equipment to keep them occupied during your temporary absence.

Ignoring your cat is a definite no-no. Not paying it mind may have it develop anxiety and an inferiority complex. Be sure that you allot a good amount of time to play and talk to your Ragamuffin each day. You want to get in touch with a vet and discuss details about the pet you intend to raise. A experienced and trusted vet will be the best person to advise you about the needs of your new pet. The vet can give you advice on its nutritional requirements, give you recommendations on how to groom your cat, advise you on brands of products to use like, soaps, shampoo, cologne, homemade equivalents, the amount of food you need to serve it at particular times of its growth as well as convenient canned foods.

It is a feline of high intelligence and a playful one at that. It plays gracefully and will not be the kind who would go into overdrive or get too hyper. Nothing is better than seeing two or more them at play. Keep in mind that a Ragamuffin stays a kitten for the first four to five years of its life, so be ready for some major cuteness overload. Just like watching babies sleep and play, you will discover yourself whiling time away just playing and observing these adorable fur balls.

Chapter Five: Acquiring Ragamuffin Cats

Finding a good breeder is what you need to do to be paired with a healthy Ragamuffin. These breeders follow a code of ethics prohibiting sales to wholesalers and pet stores. The code they observe and abide to outlines the breeder's responsibilities to buyers and their cat wards. To find breeders and to get more information about the personality and history of the ragamuffin you can check out cat association websites like the Cat Fanciers Association, the Ragamuffin Associated Group and the American Cat Fanciers Association.

Select a breeder who has completed the health certifications required to screen out genetic health problems to the fullest extent possible. You need to get in touch with a breeder who raises and keeps the kittens in their home. Isolated kittens can become skittish, fearful and may be difficult to socialize later. Run away from breeders who only seem bent in how fast they can pass on and unload a kitten on you. Turn your back on those who are more concerned about whether your credit card will go through. You also want to be able to pay a visit to their home facilities and check out with your own eyes how they interact and how the kittens respond to them.

Reputable breeders will have no problems welcoming you into their premises. Buying from a website with no possibility of seeing the pets in action leaves you very little guarantee that you will be getting what was agreed upon. Unhealthy catteries and disreputable breeders can be difficult to identify from reliable operations. There is no absolute guarantee that you won't be purchasing an ill kitten. Therefore asking the right questions, researching the breed so you understand what to expect and visiting the facilities to determine the conditions and see the animals for yourself is vital to lessen the chances of heartache, disappointment and wasted finances.

You can also pay a visit and discuss this with your veterinarian. They can usually point you to the direction of a breed rescue organization, a reputable breeder, or other trustworthy sources of healthy kittens. Put as much effort into researching your kitten as you would into picking out a new car or other big ticket purchases. Doing so will save you money in the long run. Depending on what pet you are looking for, you may have to sit it out for six months or more before the right kittens are available. So be patient. Reputable breeders typically will not hand over kittens to new people until the kittens are between 12 and 16 weeks of age.

Prior to buying a kitten, think about whether a mature Ragamuffin might be a better choice for you and your lifestyle. Kittens are buckets full of fun; however, they also entail a load of work and could be somewhat destructive until they reach a more easy-going state of adulthood. If you purchase an adult Ragamuffin, you would know more about what to expect of the cat in terms of health and personality. Should you consider getting an adult ragamuffin instead of a kitten, ask breeders about buying a retired breeding or show cat. They might even be able to tell you of an adult cat who needs a new home.

Make certain that you have a clean contract on the up and up with the rescue group, shelter or seller clearly stating the responsibilities of both breeder and buyer.

In states pet laws are murky make sure you, and the individual you acquire the cat from, are both clear on your rights and options. Whether you get a kitten or adult Ragamuffin, you will need to take your kitten/cat to the veterinarian right after adoption. Your veterinarian will be able to see problems with the feline's health, and would work with you to create a preventive regimen which will help avoid countless health issues.

Where to Acquire Your Very Own Ragamuffin Cat

Breeders aren't the only people to see to acquire a ragamuffin. You won't usually find a ragamuffin kitten in rescues or shelters but you may come across both mixed and pedigreed ragamuffins there. There are many reasons why adult pets end up in shelters and rescue facilities like divorce, death, owners relocated, illness and the list goes on. You might stumble onto good fortune and find the perfect ragamuffin for you and your family through a rescue for ragamuffin. You could also try checking your shelters in your locale or check out pet finder listings.

No matter where you get your ragamuffin, make sure that there is a written contract with the seller, shelter or rescue group is thorough and details the responsibilities of both parties. If you look up ragamuffins online you will get quite a few hits on breeders selling. It can be daunting to figure out which breeders are reputable and which ones are just in it for the money. Things like convenience, such as ability to pay online, multiple kitten availability at all times, having choices for any kitten "readily available" are some of the red flags that would identify a shady "breeder".

Save for the souls who have the ability and financial resources to take in and raise pets with illnesses, disease or deformities, most people want pets that are healthy and happy. If you are one of the latter, then doing your homework before making an acquisition is strongly advised. We have compiled a list of websites of ragamuffin breeders below:

List of Websites of Ragamuffin Cat Breeders

UNITED STATES OF AMERICA

ARIZONA

Blessed Hope Cattery

Michael & Diana Kerr

520-378-2703

Visit the cattery: http://www.blessedhopepets.com

Email: d-kerr20@live.com

Felisophic Felines

Sonya Erickson

San Tan Valley, AZ 480-529-9478

Visit the cattery: http://www.felisophic.com

Email: sonya@felisophic.com

CALIFORNIA

Teddy Bear Cats

Suzanne Young

California 818-588-0649

Visit the cattery: http://www.teddybearcats.com

Email: teddybearcats@gmail.com

COLORADO

High Country Cats

Laurie Godshall Lakewood, CO

Visit the cattery: http://www.highcountrycats.net

Email: highcountrycats@gmail.com

FLORIDA

Encore Too!

Lynn Tait

Tampa, FL 813-968-7071

Visit the cattery: http://www.encoretooragamuffin.com

Email: ikindalike@aol.com

Muffin Fantasy

Patty Ek-Collins

Altamonte Springs, FL 407-2914672

Visit the cattery: http://www.muffinfantasy.com

Email: Patty@muffinfantasy.com

ILLINOIS

Serendippity

Lynda Jay

Benton, IL 618-218-1926

Visit the cattery: http://www.serendippitymuffins.com

Email: lynda_jay@yahoo.com

Silver Linings

Stephanie & Brandon Newberry

Chicago Suburbs 815-210-1605

Visit the cattery: http://www.silverliningragamuffins.com

Email: muffinkittens@gmail.com

OKLAHOMA

Mystic Muffins

Chris Alltizer

Oklahoma City 405-888-0305

Visit the cattery: http://www.mysticmuffins.com

Email: clareleigh@aol.com

Serenity Cats

Jackie Prado

Tulsa Suburbs 918-430-8480

Visit the cattery: http://www.serenitycats.com

Email: jackie@serenitycats.com

SOUTH DAKOTA

Imperial Rags

Kristen Wiley

Northeast South Dakota 952-994-8221

Visit the cattery: http://www.imperialrags.com

Email: Kristen@imperialrags.com

TENNESSEE

RagaMuffin Cat World

Tammy Ogle

Townsend, TN 865-250-8005

Visit the cattery: http://www.ragamuffins.co

Email: Foxxmultimedia@aol.com

TEXAS

Heirloom Cats

Rebecca Jeter-Wright

Odessa/Midland 432-352-2901

Visit the cattery: http://www.heirloomcats.com

Email: Rebecca@heirloomcats.com

PANAMA

Panama RagaMuffins

Greta Lacs

Panama City +507 69484288

Email: gretalacs@gmail.com

AUSTRIA

Iris Hamertinger

Visit the Cattery: http://www.ragamuffins.at

Email: iris@ragamuffins.at

BELGIUM

'T Landthuys Erwin Hinoul & Natalie Lehaen

Visit the cattery: http://www.ragamuffin-belgischebordeaux.com

Email: cats-dogs@tlandthuys.com

HUNGARY

Amatissimi

Sylvia Bindel 0036/84-375-156

Visit the cattery: http://www.ragamuffins.eu/

Email: info@ragamuffins.eu

NETHERLANDS

Gisako RagaMuffins

Sabine Komen-Geleijn

Visit the cattery: http://www.gisako-ragamuffins.nl

Email: info@gisako-ragamuffins.nl

SWITZERLAND

Ragmopolitan

Birgit and Raphael Mahari 41-79-646-00-26

Visit the cattery: http://www.ragamuffin-cats.org

Email: momalka@bluewin

UNITED KINGDOM

WALES

Felisissimus RagaMuffins

Laura Manning Jones

Ystrad Mynach ++441443813325

Visit the cattery: http://www.ragamuffinsatfelisissimus.co.uk

Email: felisissimusrags@gmail.com

Selecting a Healthy Ragamuffin Cat

These robust cats are known to be one of the healthiest felines in the spectrum. Enjoying an average life expectancy of 10-15 years, with some noted to have lived for as long as 25 years, it is one feline who leads quite a healthy life because of their resilience and fortunate circumstance. This stroke of good genes is due to the fact that they are a naturally occurring breed, decreasing, or totally eliminating, the likelihood of genetic abnormalities that often plague other feline breeds.

You will want to deal with breeders who screen and test their cats before they release them to future guardians. Those who are upstanding in their field would have also had initial inoculation done before the cat is handed over to your eager arms.

Chapter Six: How to Feline-Proof Your Home

Felines are simply relentless when their innate curiosity is aroused. Their playful and curious nature is the basis of sayings, idioms and quotes that reference their mischief and playfulness. Cats usually get themselves in enough trouble to support these claims. Ragamuffins, even their mellow characteristic and would still have to be protected from things that could cause harm or pose danger to them.

Cat-proof your house as it will not only benefit your new Ragamuffins but also guarantees it a space that is safe, cat-worthy and feline-friendly. Doing so will also give you the peace of mind in order that you and your family live with your new Ragamuffin safely. Take stock of breakable and treasured items as you get ready to cat-proof your home.

Make mental notes of areas around your house where there may be things lying around that the new cat could play with and start making a list. Below are some reminders and tips on how to cat proof your home:

- Ragamuffins are remarkably smart felines. Keep in mind that they have keen intelligence and are highly trainable. It has been noticed that Ragamuffins learn through observation and repetition. Ragamuffins have been noted to learn opening closed doors simply by observing how their humans do this. Why do we mention this? Because your cats might get into closets where you keep dangerously toxic cleaning supplies. Avoid this by using childproof latches to keep your cat from chewing on or eating harmful chemicals.

- Save your cat a tongue-lashing and store breakable valuables away from any social area where your cat play is allowed to be in because cats are infamous explorers who thrive on satisfying their curiosity.

They will leap off and on furniture. They might knock over fragile treasures you've carefully collected accidentally. You can either box them up or store them in rooms where your Ragamuffins aren't allowed to be in.

- What may be good for us is usually not good for felines. All medicine for humans is extremely dangerous to pets if accidentally eaten. Take pains that all supplements, vitamins and medication - whether prescribed or over-the-counter - are out of your pet's reach. Make sure that pills are not left lying out where it can be found and ingested accidentally.

- Anything that mimics string can be a hazard to your playful Ragamuffins. Keep drapery ropes and blind cords coiled and away from your pet's reach. Your feline may accidentally get coiled and strangle themself or get tangled around a cord. Lessen the hazards to your Ragamuffins indoors by keeping stock of things it can mistake for playthings.

- You have to unplug electrical cords that are not in use because cats are infamous for chewing on anything stringy-looking and are easily tempted by anything that mimics string. You don't want your Ragamuffin to suffer an electric shock should it gnaw on a live wire that is plugged into live sockets. You could invest on and use commercially manufactured wire covers to protect wires from a curious cat.

- Check all unlikely nooks and crannies where your cats may want to hang out. Felines take a liking to hanging out in dark, cramped and quiet areas. Make a habit of checking washers, dryers, freezers, refrigerators, and dresser drawers. Most especially, check the underside of cars and wheels for their presence. You need to call out the cat's name when doing this. Honk the horn of your car a couple of times just to make sure your cat isn't camped out there and had fallen asleep on one of the tires while your back was turned. This is a good opportunity to remind the feline owners that your Ragamuffin is best kept and raised as an indoor cat to spare it from would be cat-thieves, larger-animal attacks, as well as getting infected with disease and illness from feral animals and MOST IMPORTANTLY vehicular accidents.

- Set out table cloths which act as an "invitation" to feline investigator. Ideally you should be able to control your cat from getting on the table - you can use a spray bottle to ward off unwanted acts from your kittens. Probability is high that kittens will try to clamber up the tablecloth and topple over whatever is set out. This could result to the shattering of your best china and an avoidable emergency trip to the vet.

- Keep toilet lids down when the toilet isn't in use. A curious kitten could fall into the bowl and not manage to climb out on its own. This is especially crucial to remember when you are at work or away from home. To avoid this, start making a habit of closing toilet covers if you haven't yet.

- We all know how awesome cats are at climbing. They may soon find their way up the kitchen sink sooner than you expect. Cats learning to do things humans do by observation can be amusing as much as dangerous. Seal up garbage disposal switches with switch boxes to keep their curious, prying paws or they might just learn how to work the garbage disposal switch and get themselves or someone else into serious trouble.

Again, we recommend that you keep and raise your Ragamuffin indoors. This is to avoid possible cat - nappers from carting your Ragamuffin away. Remember that they are friendly, trusting felines and would not know the difference of a friend or a foe unless they come across some form of trauma. You need to make sure that your window screens and screen doors do not have tears where they can slip through and exit the home. You need to have screens securely fastened and strong latches to reduce the risk of your Ragamuffin from slipping out of safety unnoticed.

Ragamuffins are happy, playful, friendly cats with a very pleasing personality given the right home and care. And even though they are remarkably well-rounded cats, it is your responsibility to understand how important it is to give it a safe haven as well as keeping your new Ragamuffins safe. Here are more tips to remember during this time of preparation of cat-proofing your home before you welcome your new Ragamuffins home:

- Store food items out of reach and sight. Keep them in locked cupboards or stack them in a closed pantry. Make certain that any food set outside of the pantry or fridge is tightly sealed in spill-proof covered containers. Calling out the name of your Ragamuffin and clapping usually does the job of dissuading it from further mischief and trouble.

- Cats are hunters by nature and will hunt, scrounge and rummage for food, fun or because of curiosity. Avoid off this natural habit of getting into places where it shouldn't by making certain your trash bins are tightly covered and won't spill out in the event of cat curiosity. This will also save you from cleaning up a mess as well as a smelly cat.

- Cats will typically play with small items that they can push around. Put away tiny valuables because your little fur ball is the sort of pet who likes to play with small, shiny objects.

- Vitamins, medication, and/or prescription drugs are to be kept away from its reach and hidden from sight. The dangers of having your Ragamuffin ingest a meant-for-human pill is the last thing you want to happen and will warrant a trip to the emergency room. The discomfort the cat has to endure to expel this from its body can be uncomfortable. Best that owners of pets avoid this preventable trip to vet by keeping all medicine locked away.
- Supplies used for cleaning the house commonly contain extremely toxic substances that can poison and make your cat very ill or worse. Keep these products out of sight and away from your Ragamuffin kitten.

- If you allow your Ragamuffin cat to wander around the house and its perimeter make sure that you do not forget to cat-proof your garage as well. Cats love to perch up on high places. Remove and hide heavy equipment or tools which they could push over the edge that might hurt them or people in the home.

- For the green thumb and those who have indoor plants or plants growing around their property, this bit is very important; there are numerous, countless plants that pose imminent danger to cats. Make sure that the greenery flanking your home are non-toxic to your Ragamuffin cat. Should you determine plants in or around your home that is toxic to your cat, think about replanting them away from the area where your cat is allowed to roam. You may also barricade these plants or replace them altogether with plants which are non-toxic to cats. Getting ill or worse from toxic plants ingestion is a very real concern and must be on top of your list of things to avoid.

- Remember that all cats tend to get swept away in the moment when they are playing. Having to deal with more than one pet can be quite a handful. To avert accidental electrocution when your felines are in a curious, playful mood or if they are rough housing with their equally furry friends, plug unused electrical sockets with plastic covers.

- It is commonly known that most kittens and cats like to gnaw on ropes, and strings. The problem is electric wires and headphone wires look like string to them. Cat-proof wires that are exposed with plastic wire coverings to avoid them from gnawing on a live wire that could get stripped off of the protective cover and cause them electrocution.

You will find several more tips and suggestions listed in this book to keep your Ragamuffin cat secure and safe within and around your home. These safety and preventive tips are aimed to benefit your friendly feline as well as you and your family in order for you to make your home safe from accidents and fairly intact. Store away things that may pose harm to your family, yourself and your cat. Doing so minimizes the possible incidence of danger to your family members.

Chapter Seven: Taking Care of Your New Ragamuffin Cat

Whether it is feline, canine, bird or reptile, understand that taking in and raising a pet entails responsibility which isn't be taken lightly. Many pet owners liken rising in pets to rearing children. Sure, not all aspects of taking care of pets or children are the same, but as parent to child and owner of pet responsibility and taking charge of situations and providing for either (or both) are constant such as identifying situations that could be dangerous have been acknowledged as similar.

Doing the necessary research to gain confidence that you and other family members know what you need to be aware of is stressed with great importance. Your readiness to take on the duties of being a pet owner will be the basis of the pet's well-being in the years to come. The thought of raising in a pet may seem easy but don't be fall prey to misleading assumptions. Raising pets successfully largely depends on the responsibility and discipline of its humans to lead a successful and healthy life.

Empower your family with crucial information and pet knowledge on what it takes and how to provide a healthy, happy and good and home life to your new loving Ragamuffin. Study up on how to set up areas and spaces for your cat. Outfit the areas of your home that will provide the Ragamuffin basic, everyday needs such as its play space, a toilet area, and a dining spot. You should also create area boundaries around your house where your cat can play in and explore under your watchful eye.

Habitat Needs for Ragamuffin Cats

Each individual kitten is different from the next one, no matter the general similarities they share. But it is safe to conclude that all cats will flourish best in homes where they are loved, wanted, cared for protected, and feel safe. In this manner, the Ragamuffin is no different from other pets.

Just because the Ragamuffin is mild-tempered and easy to deal with, generally, it is not to say that your pet won't misbehave given the proper conditions. Engaging your kittens with regular, frequent exercise and playtime is a important so that you help them channel their feisty energy that would engage them safely.

Their cuddly physical features make them quite an eye catcher and you need to protect your cat from being taken by people who may find their friendly disposition and unique size attractive to them. Trips outside the house have to be kept at a minimum and be supervised. Never let them out on their own! Keeping this standard discipline will also keep them from being attacked by wild, feral and large animal as well as catching diseases which can be passed on from a sick animal.

Keeping Your Ragamuffin Cat Healthy and Fit

Steer your Ragamuffin's playful energy with toys that will stimulate them physically and engage them mentally. The highly clever Ragamuffin is a generally trainable cat that can be trained to do tricks like retrieving toys. This is a delightful fascination of by many ragamuffin owners.

Buy them plush toys, feather teasers, lasers, and bouncy balls that would motivate them to use their energy in a positive way. If not, they could channel their energy on gnawing at you, furniture or other things around the house. Consistently be gentle when handling your kittens since felines tends to develop arthritis. Make room for a couple of scratching post and cat perches in your home so that your pet kittens are able to develop their natural climbing, leaping and scratching skills. These will also avoid home furniture from being clawed at.

Accessories and Toys for Your Ragamuffin

Ideally, your Ragamuffin should spend most of its life in the comfort and safety of your home. You should invest in amusing implements that would engage your ragamuffin kittens mentally and physically.

There are a lot of toys available out in the market to keep your cat busy and occupied while stimulating their intelligence and playful nature. There are mechanical toys your kittens can manage with simple levers like catnip sacks, chimes and bells they can tap and flick, balls that make sounds when pushed around, dvd videos of birds and fish, crinkly toys that they can toss around which produce crinkly sounds and the list just goes on. These toys are meant to engage kittens to bring out their natural traits while channeling them in positive manners with puzzle games to continuously sharpen their natural abilities.

A laser-light pointer your kittens can follow and chase after is a toy which is available almost anywhere. Using this during play can create long periods of fun and active physical exercise. Other effective entertainment tools are teasers. These are small, soft, feathery, shiny, crinkly toys attached to a string and tied on the end of a stick. This will also keep your feline fit with cardio exercises as it leaps, chase and run after a teaser. You can also make one on your own and it save a few bucks!

The Sundries You Need to Provide for Your Ragamuffin Cat

Cats like snug places. Invest well on a comfortable and warm bed for your ragamuffin to curl up into, a place to laze about or duck into when it feels like getting some alone time. If you have a porch or a big yard, set it on a soft mat or on a soft, grassy patch where it can soak up some rays and enjoy a relaxing breeze with you. A snug, warm cat bed which it can crawl into when it's spent its energy from a day of playing and bonding with you will be one of the most important furnishings you will need to purchase for your cat. A soft blanket that can also be used as a hiding place would be a nice added bonus.

Like most cats ragamuffin are some of the easiest to potty train. With that said, you still have to select and delegate spaces where your ragamuffin should go potty. Place the litter boxes of your cats in areas of the home where they go about doing their "business" in peace. Choose areas which are slightly hidden from prying eyes and place the boxes in corners around the house, like the laundry room or conceal them underneath a scratching post or cat perch.

A wise ratio of cat to litter box is 1:2. If you have more than one cat you will need more litter boxes because a cat hates nothing more than going in a dirty box and even more so when used by another cat. Not having enough litter boxes to go around may get the cat constipated as it might hold it in. Two litter boxes for each feline you have ensures that the feline will not become constipated. This can be avoided by regular litter box cleaning or when needed.

There are so many brand choices of scented cat litter available that will help keep litter box cleanliness in check. Make sure that each litter box is clean out when needed at all times. You want clear a soiled litter box as soon as you can. Make sure that you check on its cleanliness routinely at least twice a day. Doing so will ensure that your Ragamuffin will have no reservations about answering to nature's call.

Another useful equipment to invest on and which you will often use is a good, strong brush or comb. A brush is a tool you can use to bond with you ragamuffin. A good brushing will not only strengthen your bond with your cat, but it will also aid the circulation of essential skin oils to keep its in good condition. A durable and sturdy cat-crate or carrier is what you will need for out-of-town trips, holidays and family vacations. It can also be used as a transportable cat bed during extended trips away from home. A carrier or crate will also come in handy for quick errands around your local neighborhood. Make sure to lay down a familiar blanket which has a homey scent to lessen the impact of being in an unfamiliar place.

Plastic feeding dishes are inferior, wear out easily, can be toxic and difficult to clean. Instead choose stainless steel or ceramic feeding dishes for your cat's water and food. Ceramic and stainless steel bowls are easier to clean, are not made of toxic materials, do not retain food smell and are safer for your cats.

Just like most cats, dental hygiene is important for ragamuffins because felines are prone to periodontal disease and mouth infections. Avoid these by brushing their teeth on a monthly basis. You can get the help of your vet or a cat groomer and set monthly appointments with them. Ask your groomer or vet to show you how to brush your cat's teeth correctly. Once you have observed the procedure often enough you can save some money and do it yourself at home.

Place your money on durable equipment and grooming supplies. Making an investment in the more sturdy equipment is important or you will be spending much more money for sundries that are inferior and won't last long. You and your cat will need many of these equipment and tools and will serve both of you well for a long time, if you make that invest wisely.

The Health of a Ragamuffin Cat

Every living being has a potential to inherit disease and develop genetic issues regarding its health. If a breeder has no evidence that they have taken all the proper steps on vaccinating their temporary wards before handing the cats to you, you need to turn away fast. If a breeder cannot give you a health guarantee on the kittens they take that as a red flag and look elsewhere. Any breeder who verbally tells you that the kittens are a hundred percent healthy with no possible or foreseeable health problems is a no - no.

The Ragamuffin has a rectangular shaped head that rests on a short neck. It is a muscular cat. It is born white and develops its various colors and patterns as it matures. It has medium to long coat and lengthens toward its belly area.

Its thick, plush fur is easy to manage with regular grooming. It does not tend to mat, tangle or clump. It takes about five years for a Ragamuffin to mature so you will be sure to enjoy kitten madness for quite a while. These felines are generally hardy cats; however hereditary health problems which can be a concern are polycystic kidney disease and hypertrophic cardiomyopathy.

The most common form of heart disease in cats is hypertrophic cardiomyopathy (HCM) . This causes hypertrophy or thickening of the cat's heart muscle. An echocardiogram exam can detect and confirm if a cat has HCM. The genetic mutation that results in the development of HCM in the Ragamuffin's has been identified by researchers and has developed a genetic test which gives breeders the edge. Breeders are now able to screen cats before breeding them. Cats with HCM must be taken out of breeding programs. Stay away from breeders who say they have HCM-free lines. No breeder can give a guarantee that their cats will not develop HCM.

Ancestry plays a large role in the future good health of a Ragamuffin. Because of its Persian ancestry some

Ragamuffins are prone to renal failure which is medically called polycystic kidney disease. Thankfully, there are genetic exams available these days which can help identify if a cat is affected with PKD or is a carrier.

Ask the breeder to present proof that a kitten's parents were screened for HCM and PKD and do not by any means do business with a breeder who can't come up with a guarantee in writing.

Grooming

The Ragamuffin sports a medium to medium-long fur with a silky, soft texture. Its coat does not typically tangle or mat and is quite easy to manage. However, ragamuffins who have Persians ancestry in their pedigree could mat more than others. Invest a stainless steel comb and a flexible rubber-like brush to comb or brush out its coat at least twice a week. Do this during downtime, typically after a good play period when it is relaxed and ready to join you for a cuddle and it will truly enjoy the loving attention. Like all felines, the coat of the ragamuffin sheds, but not to excess.

Apart from the twice weekly grooming the three other grooming it requires is getting its ears cleaned and trimming its nails. Clip the nails as needed or once every two weeks. To do this you want to gently press on the paws and cut above the quick. Do not cut too deeply as this may cause profuse bleeding.

Clean out its ears as needed and use a cotton ball moistened with some warm water. Never employ cotton buds on a stick as this may injure your cat. All felines have a tendency to get periodontal disease so it is important that you give your cat a good tooth brushing using toothpaste recommended by vets and is pet approved.

You may give your Ragamuffin a good wipe down with a vet-approved wipes when it needs it. This is usually after meal time when it may get food debris caught on its whiskers. Cats are usually good at getting those by self-cleaning, but you want to make sure that no food is stuck on its face.

Chapter Eight: The Nutritional Needs of Your Ragamuffin Cat

Like other pets, and people, your Ragamuffin will be at its healthiest and thrive best physically and mentally if given proper nutrition. Therefore you must choose the right kinds of foods which would meet your Ragamuffin's nutritional requirements. Keep in mind that your Ragamuffin is one of the best of feline breeds and least likely to be prone to most feline illnesses. With this in mind you will be more confident knowing that raising two or more ragamuffins will not be complicated as long as you provide it with a proper and balanced diet each time.

Diet Basics

Picking out the proper foods to feed your ragamuffin cat will be very important to its continued wellbeing and good health, both mentally and physically. These days, cat owners have a better advantage and a vast number of food choices when choosing what sort of foods to feed their pets. Study up and empower yourself on what ingredients pet food producers use to make their products. Learn to decipher and read complicated-sounding ingredients printed on food labels. Get familiar with the wordings and jargons food manufacturers use to sell their products.

Ask your ragamuffin cat breeder for their recommendations and the preference of your cat whilst they were with them. Talk to your ragamuffin health provider about your cat's diet and have the vet determine which kinds of foods are best for the nutrition for your cats.

The Balanced Nourishment Your Ragamuffin Cat Needs

In order to raise a healthy and happy ragamuffin, serving up optimum, healthy food that gives it a balanced diet and proper nutritional needs is very important. When picking out food for your Ragamuffin, make sure that the packaging states it meets the guidelines stated by the

American Association of Feed Control Officials (AAFCO). This certifies that the food product meets at least the minimum dietary requirements of your Ragamuffin.

Like other felines, Ragamuffins are predators. Always keep that in mind when you consider what you must serve and feed to your Ragamuffin. If you veer from this fact, your Ragamuffin may appear like it was a picky eater. If you give your kittens non-meat based foods like seeds, fruits, dairy, vegetables, nuts, rice, etc., you might find it difficult to get the Ragamuffin to eat.

The diet of a ragamuffin is not difficult to meet, too expensive nor does it require anything out of the ordinary in its diet. In a nutshell, they have no unusual dietary needs that should be added to their nutrition. Ragamuffin is hearty, eager eaters and once you understand which food they like, they are not picky about the kind of food given to them. They are commonly happy with their favorite sort of food and would usually ask for a second helping. Felines are good at convincing their owners that that they haven't been fed enough and would typically beg for more. As long as you have given them their proper portion and share for that meal, try not give in. In fact, resist. Felines will almost always try to get their way by asking for more and if you give in to its convincing pity-me eyes, you will be complicit to it forming a bad habit of eating more than it should which can lead to obesity and a less active lifestyle.

Cats who suffer from obesity have a tendency to having joint and bone problems because of the excess weight they carry around. This may lead to the cat not wanting to play or move. Jumping could become a problem for them as they will have to cushion their fall on small paws that can't bear the weight the heavy landing. Owners of cats are advised to feed their ragamuffin kittens small meals according to its weight. Frequency of feeding should be three separate meals throughout the day. After the seventh month you may increase the portions, again according to weight and activity level, but cut down the feeding frequency to two times a day.

Seasoned caregivers and expert breeders of ragamuffins suggest feeding your cats a high-grade, dry cat food, ideally grain free. Grain free foods contain more filler in the recipe, so there are more unusable nutrients mixed into the meals. This may be more expensive when compared to supermarket brands but will benefit your cat more health wise in the long run. A healthy cat equates to a strong one not needing constant medical care, which equates to a happy feline and whole lot of savings. One other benefit to feeding your cat premium dry cat food is fewer feces to scoop out of your cat's litter box.

Kinds of Food to Feed Your Ragamuffin Cats

The continued good health of your ragamuffins will save you from paying for expensive pet health care leaving you with a bigger budget to buy optimum, quality food to serve up to your cats. Since ragamuffins have no special requirement in food, apart from having a balanced diet determining how to give them that will be your job to learn. Your ragamuffins will be able to get all their nutritional requirements if you pay mind to provide them proper optimum pet food. Giving your ragamuffins the right kinds of good quality pet food shall supply the cats all the nutrients, minerals and vitamins it would need to enjoy good health and happily thrive. As your ragamuffins get older you will want to add more food to each meal but lessen meal frequency from three to two meals a day.

Reading Labels and Foods Ingredients to Avoid

Do not buy any food products labeled "meals" and/or "by-products". These products are made from dubious meat parts rejected from already-processed meats, not fit for human consumption and end up in pet foods. These questionable "meat" ingredients are unusable parts gotten from a pig, chicken or cow tossed aside after processing food for human consumption. These parts are usually chicken leg stems, feet, head or beak. These are cow intestines, lungs, nose, tongue, hoof, tail, cheek, or ear. These could also contain pig snout, hoof, tail, face and skin. The list of possible rejected animal parts continues.

In order to mask the low-grade quality and inferiority of pet food products, additives are used in the recipe. Most preservatives are carcinogenic when ingested by humans. Preservatives are used to produce pet food in order to limit bacteria growth and/or inhibit food oxidation. Do not buy pet food products that contain preservatives like sodium nitrate, nitrate, BHT, and BHA. In order to entice would be buyers into making a purchase artificial coloring is used, but keep in mind, that artificial coloring may be the reason for allergic reactions in pets and provide no nutritional value to them.

Keep in mind that picking out the proper sort of food that is good for your pet's health is your responsibility. Your cat won't know the difference or bother how the food looks, only how it tastes.

Home Cooked or Branded? What to Feed Your Ragamuffin Cats

Keep in mind that your cat is a meat-eater. Attempting to have it eat fruits, rice, nuts, or vegetables will not be sufficient for it. Many seasoned ragamuffin owners agree that one of the best food variant choices for your cat pets is prime, dry cat food. It not only provides a good, balanced meal for your ragamuffin, it also helps clean the teeth of your cat and in addition, keeps longer enjoying an extended shelf life. The next choice of suitable food that will sustain all your ragamuffins' nutritional requirements would be prime grade cat food. Just mix in a little bit of water and you are good to go. With a clear expiry date, it may not last as long as dry food and canned food needs to be consumed immediately one out of the can, but it will do the job of providing a balanced meal for your ragamuffin.

Alternately you may want to consider giving your cat's home cooked meals. There are pros and cons to choosing this method of feeding. You will have to factor in an additional expense on top of your food list every month. You will have to shop for fresh food, make sure that the meals you cook up for your cats are balanced and meet all nutritional needs, and this will take more time from your regular schedule. This method requires measuring ingredients mindfully. The pros of this method really are just looking at the cons and make them work for you.

Clean Water

Cats aren't famous water drinkers and will probably have to be coaxed to drinking fresh water. It is important that your cat pet replenish its lost fluids and drink up. Upon observing felines it had been noted that they have a preference for drinking running water such as from a fountain. Not all of us will have a stream running through neither our backyard nor a drinking fountain, but if you can fashion something like it, it would be optimal. No matter what always be sure to leave a fresh bowl of clean water for your cats.

Food Additives

Food additives present in any store bought pet meal must be avoided by any potential ragamuffin owner. You will need to develop effective shopping skills to understand how manufacturers label their products because there are additives that are put into recipes to enhance quality and there are those which serve as fillers with no nutritional value. Make it a point to understand how to read labels in order to confidently serve the right sort of food to your pet.

Tips for Selecting a High-Quality Cat Food Brand

Don't get carried away by marketing hype instead learn to decipher food labels and nutritional values. Get to know what they mean so you only serve up healthy servings to your cats eat time. Almost all expensive brands would say they only use quality meats and produce in their recipes. However you can't rely on that because premium or gourmet pet foods are not compelled to use better ingredients than less expensive yet complete in nutritional value food products. Food labels claiming to contain "natural" ingredients are gained from mined, plant or animal sources. These natural foods should not have artificial products like coloring, preservatives or artificial flavors. Nor should natural food be overly processed.

Pet foods that are produced without the use of conventional pesticides or artificial fertilizers are labeled "organic". Only meats from animals that were raised without the use of growth hormones or the use of antibiotics and were fed healthy organic diets are included in the recipe. Buyer be aware that organic foods are graded differently. Labels boasting a particular percentage of organic ingredients are the basis of the grade. Organic foods are not contaminated by industrial or human wastes. Food additives are not added in organic foods nor does it go through ionizing radiation.

How Much to Feed Your Ragamuffin

You will have to do some experimenting at the onset to determine the kind of canned or premium dry foods your kitten will take a liking to, so buy small sacks and a couple of cans at the beginning. You will be able to determine which foods your cats prefer immediately by observing their gusto or lack thereof for the food. You can also tell this by observing the feline's body language when it gets a whiff of what you are serving. Look for other brands and food sorts if your ragamuffin doesn't eat too much. Not having enough food will lead to ill health due to malnourishment.

In order to find out how much food you should serve your cats each time, experiment by giving it 2 cups of premium dry food. Set out the dish for 30 minutes and allow it to eat within that amount of time. Subtract the measure of the leftover food from the original 2 cups and the sum is what your cat is able to eat during meals. Repeat this measuring method for the next 2-3 days so that you get an accurate reading of the amount of food your kitten is able to eat.

Give your young ragamuffins 3 small meals a day until it is 7 months old. As your ragamuffins mature, you should increase the amount of food you set out for it while reducing the frequency of feeding. Adult cats do not have to feed as often as kittens. Be careful of the amount of food you serve a more mature kitten to avoid over feeding and food wastage.

Chapter Nine: Information on Basic Cat Breeding

Breeding cats may seem simple enough, right? But that isn't quite the case. It takes more than throwing a male and a female together to develop a good litter of kittens. To be a thoughtful breeder of Ragamuffins, you would need the mindset of developing the breed too. You not only want a successful mating which leads to pregnancy, but also healthy, and even-tempered kittens. To satisfy the correct breeding procedures you first need to discuss the topic of breeding with your vet because your pet's doctor can guide you and take the necessary steps to examine your cat and determine its health. You will also need to talk about the proper diet for your cat as much of its requirements will change and some would need to be increased. Should you have a purebred cat, you will have to get your cat examined and tested for the possibilities of inherited diseases and medical conditions which it may pass down to the litter. This is one crucial point of breeding to meet the ethical standards of breeding the lovable Ragamuffin.

Your ragamuffin's doctor is one of the best candidates to determine common medical issues which your cat may be prone to. They will be able to conduct the appropriate tests to figure out if the cats intended to mate are sound breeding candidates. Another person who will be able to answer the questions about the cat's history is the breeder who you dealt with during acquisition. This is why it is important that you work with an upstanding breeder at the onset of acquiring your cat, because a reputable breeder would have taken all the initial measures to ensure a healthy litter.

A cat's temperament is an important factor to determine before even thinking about breeding it. If a cat that is overly shy, aggressive or highly anxious they are usually not very good candidates to be parent because chances are they will pass down these traits to their offspring. Selecting the mate has to be carried out thoughtfully with utter consideration. You need to find and choose alone for your cat to breed with who complements your cats own traits as well as physical characteristics, like structure, health, color and temperament. This is where your breeder comes to play as they would be able to help you identify your cat's weaknesses and strengths.

Purebred felines acknowledged and recognized by various cat societies and associations have set standards to meet. These standards are written and followed in order to keep the pedigree as pure as possible and to ensure that the kittens enjoy good health. As owner to the ragamuffins you intend to breed you will need to take the time to study the breed standards of your ragamuffin to evaluate its consistency or lack thereof with the breeding standard and to determine if your cat is suitable for breeding.

Mating Behavior of Cats

Female cats or queens go through four hormonal cycles which indicate mating behavior for the feline. During this time of the mating cycle which lasts 10-14 days, the ready to mate will begin to display mating behaviors so as to attract a tomcat. This mating behavior is recognized in stages. Stage one is when the feline shall start to rub her head and neck on anything she can come into contact with. She could be unusually quiet or extremely vocal during this first stage. She will also consume more food than usual and shall appear to be a bit more restless. She will call out and attract tom cats and be quite selective with her choices notably refusing advances of most toms and would opt to get to know the male cats first before making her choice.

Your female cat may also urinate around the house and 'mark' spots. Once she makes a decision about a suitable tom she will go to great and extreme lengths to catch its attention. This is usually a short stage and goes unnoticed to the untrained eye. If you do not want your female cat to get pregnant you can prevent this by getting her spayed or keep her indoors and away from male cats. However this period of heat shall happen again and she will go through the usual stages of yowling and urinating in the house again. To avoid that you need to determine if you want to breed her. If not then you have to get her neutered.

The next and second stage is when you will detect and see signs of cat heat behavior. Stage one signs previously discussed will all be noted but with extreme intensity. This is when you will notice and hear loud vocalization from her to call out to her chosen partner. She may appear to be more affectionate and want to be beside you more often, however she would not want to be touched, picked up or handled at this time. You will notice your female feline crouch down on her front legs as she stretches her back, hyper extending it to expose her vulva as an indication of readiness to mate.

A good way of telling this is to test by stroking your cat's tail. Should she lift her back and put her tail to the side this shows that she is most likely in heat. If the female was not engaged in any mating activity with a male cat the cycle begins again and during this third stage the female cat will not have any desire to meet with any male cats at all. The fourth stage lasts for a period of 90 days anywhere between November through January and this is supposed to be due to shorter days of the year.

Female Mating Behavior

When your queen or female cat is ready to mate, she will start to get friendlier with the male cat she seems to be a worthy partner. Both of the cats shall start sniffing and exploring each other's bodies and would appear to be kissing as they include each other's faces during this time of exploring. You would notice each of them lick each other and sniff each other's sexual organs. This is the manner that makes the female cat aroused. When arousal is apparent, the female cat shall move into a crouching position moving its tail to its side allowing maximum exposure of its vulva. This is when you know that a female cat is ready to have sexual contact. If the female is not ready for the mounting stage where the tom begins to copulate with her, the mating process will have a violent outcome for both of the cats.

This happens when the female cat is in the middle of the "heat" cycle and not ready yet nor is it willing to welcome the tom - or the first stage. Female cats have been noted and seen to scratch at and bite a tom cat to keep it away from her when she isn't ready quite yet to be mounted. Female feline are very decisive with the tom cat they chose to mate with and would refuse at all costs - the advances of a male cat you might pair her up with. The violence is more notable when they are 'forced" to mate by an eager feral tom.

Tom Cat Mounting Behavior

When the tom cat notices a female in heat - whether in the wild or in arranged conditions, the tom will put his fore paws on both sides of the queen while it takes hold of the female cat's neck by biting on it with its teeth. The tom will begin to move himself up and down on the prose female using its hind feet. He then introduces his to the entrance of the vulva and begins to enter it until the tom releases and ejaculates. The introduced penis of the tom shall then stimulate the inner female parts of the cat or the vagina, and will cause the female cat to ovulate. The female cat shall then let out a loud, shrill yowl and will quickly pull and move away from the male cat. The tom cat's penis, having sharp edges shall very likely cause the female to feel pain.

Both of the mating cats could go through the process again in order to make sure that the female cat's ovulation had been stimulated successfully. A female cat which just copulated with a tom cat should not to be moved or touched until she has finished the final phase of the feline ritual of mating which will be indicated by her grooming herself. The self-grooming process happens right after she has been mounted.

Chapter Ten: Ragamuffin Cat Standards, Registration and Breeding

All purebreds acknowledged and recognized by various cat clubs have physical standards that should be mindfully considered since the goal of breeding kittens is to better the breed. Study the standard guides of your pet feline and assess your cat against the standard. You should look for a mate that best complements your pet feline's size, temperament, structure, structure and color to achieve a cat worthy for a show and as a breeding stock.

Breed Standards of the Ragamuffin Cat

The CFA Ragamuffin Standard

GENERAL

The Ragamuffin is a big breed of cat that is equally well balanced in physical characteristics and personality. While their sweet characteristic is due to their shape, size, and their expressive eyes along with puffy whisker pads, none of these physical characteristic should be extreme. It is a sturdy cat with bones uniform with its size. It becomes fully mature when it reaches four years old. While the ragamuffin breed is a huge cat, females may be considerably smaller than males. Both male and female must be heavy and muscular with a dense pad on the lower abdomen. Ragamuffins are engulfed in rich coats of almost every pattern and color, with the welcomed and occasional look of a white tipped tail. Ragamuffins are bred to be intelligent, affectionate, sociable and cuddly companions that are entertaining and playful throughout their lives.

HEAD

The size and shape of the Ragamuffin's head is a modified broad wedge. It has a rounded appearance.

The forehead must be slightly rounded. Its head is medium-sized, and in proportion with the body; the image is softened by the fur surrounding it. The Ragamuffin's muzzle is rounded, and a bit shorter in length, highlighting the width of the head. Its whisker pad is puffy, and gives it its characteristic sweet look. The cheeks of the Ragamuffin are full. Seen from profile, its chin is round. The cat's nose dips giving the effect of an even scoop, and trails gently graceful curved forehead and top of head.

The Ragamuffin's neck is brief, strong and heavy, especially in older males. An allocation is made for loose-jowls in mature males. The Ragamuffin's ears must be set equally on the side of its head as on top. Its ears are to be medium in size, rounded, and slightly tipped forward, with average furnishings. They must in harmonious proportion to its head. Ear tufts are acceptable. Its large expressive eyes are walnut shaped and, adequately wide set. A slight oriental taper to the eye is allowed. The more vivid the eye color, the better. A lighter eye color shade in dilutes is acceptable. Eye color regulations are as follows:

Eye Color Requirements

Blue eyes and Color Points: Odd Eyes, Blue, Blue/Green, Green, Green/Blue, Aqua, Minks. For Sepias,

Odd Eyes, Gold/Green, Gold, to Green/Gold. All colors in Silvers and Solids are acceptable.

Note: The walnut shaped eyes of the ragamuffin are best seen at eye level. When observed from high with the cat looking up the shape appears rounder than walnut in shape.

Body

The ragamuffin's body is rectangular with broad shoulders and a wide chest. It is slightly heavy muscled in the back-legs with hindquarters equally as wide as the shoulders. There must be a floppy patch of skin in the cat's lower belly area. These cats are heavily fleshed. Its ribs and backbone must not be obvious to the eye. Upon palpation these areas must feel fully covered with flesh. Full adulthood is attained at four years of age. At this stage of its life the ragamuffin is occasionally described to be Rubenesque.

Tail

Its long tail is proportioned to the body and is fully furred, much like a bottlebrush or plume. It is soft, with medium density at the base and a slight taper at the tip.

Legs and Paws

Its heavily boned legs should be medium to medium-long in measure with its hind legs a bit longer than its forelegs, but is with proportion to its body. The paws of the ragamuffin must be round and large. All four paws must be able to carry the weight of the ragamuffin without splaying. There should be tufts under and between the paws.

Coat

Its Fur is medium to medium-long in length. The texture must be silky, soft and dense. Coat texture will differ a bit according to color. Its fur length must be a tad longer in the neck area as well as the extremities of its face giving it the appearance of a ruff, and should increase in length from the top of its head all the way down through to its shoulder blades and back. The coat on its sides and stomach area must have medium to medium-long fur. The fur on the forelegs must dense with short to medium length. The fur on its back legs must be medium to medium-long in length and should be dense giving it the look of a wispy frill on its hindquarters.

Color

All patterns and colors is allowed whether with or without white. Any extent of white fur is allowed as with white spots on back, belly, paws or chest; a locket, a blaze, white tip on tail, etc. The mark of evenness, whether in the white spotting or the pattern, is not important. All colors are accepted of its paw pads and nose leather and in any combination of color, not particularly related to its coat color. Ragamuffins with white on its feet could have pink paw pads or they could be multicolored or bicolored. Body darkening in older cats is allowed as well as incomplete or lighter markings in kittens. The Ragamuffins are famous for being easy-going felines that are easy to handle, even if handled by strangers. While a few of them could get upset by surroundings and slightly complain, they are not to try to scratch or bite the handler or Judge.

Allowances

Head area: soft features in females; not fully developed eye color in young cats, especially minks.
Body area: fatty pad which are not fully developed in young cats; lighter-weighing young full cats; finer bones in females.
Coat: Short or lack of ruff on full cats and kittens; shorter fur on legs of the cats that have medium coat; seasonal changes in coat color and length; darker body color in older cats.
Preferences are given to a cat with an affectionate nature and deep, bright colored eyes.

Individual Registration

The formal request for registration to register your Ragamuffin with the Cat Fancier's Association shall have to come from the breeder. You have to get in touch with the breeder and request for the Application for Registry which is also referred to as a "blue slip." You have to be mindful that a good breeder could choose to hold back the release of the application for registry if your purchase contract states that the kitten has to be neutered or spayed before the registration application is given over to you. This is typical practice for upstanding breeders of pedigreed cats. If the condition for registry is not met from your end, the CFA can do nothing until the terms of the sales contract is satisfied.

In order for the CFA to grant registration to a feline without the standard application form, ancillary papers have to be provided along with a request letter to CFA. The supporting papers required are the following; a pedigree or another ancillary document provided by the breeder establishing the cat's qualifications to be registered under the Cat Fanciers Association. The birth date of the cat and its parent's registration numbers with the CFA, further information if the cat was purchased with or without breeding permissions should be provided too. In lieu of this, you may furnish a copy of the written purchase contract that states the circumstances of the transaction. This has to be signed by all the involved parties. This contract between the parties must state that CFA documents must be given. The date of birth and CFA registration numbers of the kitten's parents being registered has to be stated as well whether the feline was purchased with or without the permission to breed.

Upon receiving these documents, the Central Office shall reach out and contact the breeder and request for their cooperation and/or remarks to fast track the decision of the matter. In the event of incomplete submission of documents or data that are not stated in these records, the Central Office will not be able to provide any assistance.

This would be a good time to remind you to clarify the details of your contract with the breeder you will be dealing with. Figure out early if you want the female feline to mate and breed in the future. Making the decision about this detail early allows you to discuss and decide about this with your breeder. Have all the proper paperwork transfer hands and document all ancillary details (record of screening tests, down payment and purchase receipts, certifications, etc.) filed away and ready at a moment's notice.

For the CFA to register a cat with breeding rights there should be a PIN noted and present on the blue slip given by the breeder. This PIN can be found in the PIN box of the blue slip or the Application for Registration. It is a random, 5-digit, computer-generated number that will be present only on the Certificate of Litter Registration provided to the breeder.

For each litter registered, a PIN is assigned only to that particular litter. Only the breeder of the litter shall have access to this PIN - there will be no record of this number with the CFA. If the cat was previously filed with the CFA as a not for breeding cat, you will have to contact the breeder to ask for the Litter PIN. You will have to write down the PIN on the certificate of registration and submit it to the CFA with a specified request to change the NFB status registration to a breed cat. The payment for this correction is $15.00.

Basic Cat Breeding Information for Show

Before you consider breeding your Ragamuffin, you have to find out about the breeding basics of cats to ensure a successful result. It is vital that you talk about this with your vet since your pet's doctor can take stock and check if the health of your feline is good for breeding. As about the correct diet for pregnant cats as some nutritional needs will have to be increased or added. If your Ragamuffin is purebred, or has Persian ancestry, you should talk about possible health conditions which could have been inherited. Since the Ragamuffin is a developed breed and could have Persian genes, the likelihood of it inheriting a disease from its mother and father could be possible but slim. Still, this doesn't mean you should forgo discussing ethical procedures of breeding.

Your pet physician should be able to determine what medical issues are common with the specific breed of your cat. Your vet can also figure out if your cat is a right candidate to breed. An important factor to consider is the temperament of the cat. This is a factor to consider because it will be a foreboding of the temperament of the litter it produces. A cat that is overly aggressive, shy, anxious, or highly nervous are usually poor candidates to be parents because they pass down this negative traits to their offspring.

Mate selection for the cat must be done with great consideration, thought and care. Select a mate who best complements your physical characteristics and pet's temperament. Ask for the advice of an experienced breeder to help you identify your cat's weaknesses and strengths.

Abundism – Referring to a cat that has markings more prolific than is normal.

Acariasis – A type of mite infection.

ACF – Australian Cat Federation

Affix – A cattery name that follows the cat's registered name; cattery owner, not the breeder of the cat.

Agouti – A type of natural coloring pattern in which individual hairs have bands of light and dark coloring.

Ailurophile – A person who loves cats.

Albino – A type of genetic mutation which results in little to no pigmentation, in the eyes, skin, and coat.

Allbreed – Referring to a show that accepts all breeds or a judge who is qualified to judge all breeds.

Alley Cat – A non-pedigreed cat.

Alter – A desexed cat; a male cat that has been neutered or a female that has been spayed.

Amino Acid – The building blocks of protein; there are 22 types for cats, 11 of which can be synthesized and 11 which must come from the diet (see essential amino acid).

Anestrus – The period between estrus cycles in a female cat.

Any Other Variety (AOV) – A registered cat that doesn't conform to the breed standard.

ASH – American Shorthair, a breed of cat.

Back Cross – A type of breeding in which the offspring is mated back to the parent.

Balance – Referring to the cat's structure; proportional in accordance with the breed standard.

Barring – Describing the tabby's striped markings.

Base Color – The color of the coat.

Bicolor – A cat with patched color and white.

Blaze – A white coloring on the face, usually in the shape of an inverted V.

Bloodline – The pedigree of the cat.

Brindle – A type of coloring, a brownish or tawny coat with streaks of another color.

Castration – The surgical removal of a male cat's testicles.

Cat Show – An event where cats are shown and judged.

Cattery – A registered cat breeder; also, a place where cats may be boarded.

CFA – The Cat Fanciers Association.

Cobby – A compact body type.

Colony – A group of cats living wild outside.

Color Point – A type of coat pattern that is controlled by color point alleles; pigmentation on the tail, legs, face, and ears with an ivory or white coat.

Colostrum – The first milk produced by a lactating female; contains vital nutrients and antibodies.

Conformation – The degree to which a pedigreed cat adheres to the breed standard.

Cross Breed – The offspring produced by mating two distinct breeds.

Dam – The female parent.

Declawing – The surgical removal of the cat's claw and first toe joint.

Developed Breed – A breed that was developed through selective breeding and crossing with established breeds.

Down Hairs – The short, fine hairs closest to the body which keep the cat warm.

DSH – Domestic Shorthair.

Estrus – The reproductive cycle in female cats during which she becomes fertile and receptive to mating.

Fading Kitten Syndrome – Kittens that die within the first two weeks after birth; the cause is generally unknown.

Feral – A wild, untamed cat of domestic descent.

Gestation – Pregnancy; the period during which the fetuses develop in the female's uterus.

Guard Hairs – Coarse, outer hairs on the coat.

Harlequin – A type of coloring in which there are van markings of any color with the addition of small patches of the same color on the legs and body.

Inbreeding – The breeding of related cats within a closed group or breed.

Kibble – Another name for dry cat food.

Lilac – A type of coat color that is pale pinkish-gray.

Line – The pedigree of ancestors; family tree.

Litter – The name given to a group of kittens born at the same time from a single female.

Mask – A type of coloring seen on the face in some breeds.

Matts – Knots or tangles in the cat's fur.

Mittens – White markings on the feet of a cat.

Moggie – Another name for a mixed breed cat.

Mutation – A change in the DNA of a cell.

Muzzle – The nose and jaws of an animal.

Natural Breed – A breed that developed without selective breeding or the assistance of humans.

Neutering – Desexing a male cat.

Open Show – A show in which spectators are allowed to view the judging.

Pads – The thick skin on the bottom of the feet.

Particolor – A type of coloration in which there are markings of two or more distinct colors.

Patched – A type of coloration in which there is any solid color, tabby, or tortoiseshell color plus white.

Pedigree – A purebred cat; the cat's papers showing its family history.

Pet Quality – A cat that is not deemed of high enough standard to be shown or bred.

Piebald – A cat with white patches of fur.

Points – Also color points; markings of contrasting color on the face, ears, legs, and tail.

Pricked – Referring to ears that sit upright.

Purebred – A pedigreed cat.

Queen – An intact female cat.

Roman Nose – A type of nose shape with a bump or arch.

Scruff – The loose skin on the back of a cat's neck.

Selective Breeding – A method of modifying or improving a breed by choosing cats with desirable traits.

Senior – A cat that is more than 5 but less than 7 years old.

Sire – The male parent of a cat.

Solid – Also self; a cat with a single coat color.

Spay – Desexing a female cat.

Stud – An intact male cat.

Tabby – A type of coat pattern consisting of a contrasting color over a ground color.

Tom Cat – An intact male cat.

Tortoiseshell – A type of coat pattern consisting of a mosaic of red or cream and another base color.

Tri-Color – A type of coat pattern consisting of three distinct colors in the coat.

Tuxedo – A black and white cat.

Unaltered – A cat that has not been desexed.

INDEX

A

B

C

D

E

F

G

H

I

J

K

L

M

N

O

P

R

S

T

Photo Credits

Page Photo by user Togle1 via Wikimedia Commons, https://commons.wikimedia.org/wiki/File:Ragamuffin_kitten-GRACIE.png

Page Photo by user Takashi Hososhima via Wikimedia Commons, https://commons.wikimedia.org/wiki/File:Ramu_(6873201112).jpg

Page Photo by user Takashi Hososhima via Wikimedia Commons, https://commons.wikimedia.org/wiki/File:What_are_you_up_to%3F_(7750736126).jpg

Page Photo by user Togle1 via Wikimedia Commons, https://commons.wikimedia.org/wiki/File:RagaMuffin_Kitten.png

Page Photo by user Teddy Llovet via Flickr.com, https://www.flickr.com/photos/teddyllovet/5596909699/

Page Photo by user Teddy Llovet via Flickr.com, https://www.flickr.com/photos/teddyllovet/13686666604/

Page Photo by user Saiphfire via Flickr.com, https://www.flickr.com/photos/saiphfire/828803620/

Page Photo by user Teddy Llovet via Flickr.com, https://www.flickr.com/photos/teddyllovet/4498829563/

Page Photo by user Alan L. via Flickr.com, https://www.flickr.com/photos/35188692@N00/82914624/

Page Photo by user Teddy Llovet via Flickr.com, https://www.flickr.com/photos/teddyllovet/4000506634/

References

"Breed Profile: Ragamuffin" CFA.org
http://www.cfa.org/Breeds/BreedsKthruR/Ragamuffin.aspx

"Breed Standard" Ragamuffingroup.com
http://www.ragamuffingroup.com/breed-standard/

"Cat Breeds Getting Cats to Get Along" Petcarerx.com
https://www.petcarerx.com/article/cat-breeds-getting-cats-to-get-along/825

"Differences between Ragdoll & Ragamuffin Cats" The Nest
http://pets.thenest.com/differences-between-ragdoll-ragamuffin-cats-4809.html

"Ragdoll or Ragamuffin?" PetMd.com

http://www.petmd.com/cat/breeds/c_ct_ragdoll

"Ragamuffin" Vetstreet.com

http://www.vetstreet.com/cats/ragamuffin#upper-tabs

"Ragamuffin" Animal Planet

https://www.animalplanet.com/tv-shows/cats-101/videos/ragamuffin

"Ragamuffin Care" Blessedhopepets.com

http://www.blessedhopepets.com/ragamuffin-care

"Ragamuffin Cat" Petful.com

http://www.petful.com/cat-breeds/profile-ragamuffin/

"Ragamuffin Cat" Wikipedia.com

https://en.wikipedia.org/wiki/Ragamuffin_cat

"Ragamuffin Cat Breed" Pawculture.com

http://www.pawculture.com/breed-basics/cat-breeds/ragamuffin-cat-breed/

"Ragamuffin Cat Breed History" Ragamuffingroup.com
http://www.ragamuffingroup.com/breed-history

"Ragamuffin Kittens" Imperial Rags
http://www.imperialrags.com/adoption_info

"What Do Ragamuffins Eat?" Animal Care Tip
http://animalcaretip.com/what-do-ragamuffins-eat-2/

"Who Has Kittens?" Ragamuffingroup.com
http://www.ragamuffingroup.com/breeders-kitten-availability/

Feeding Baby
Cynthia Cherry
978-1941070000

Axolotl
Lolly Brown
978-0989658430

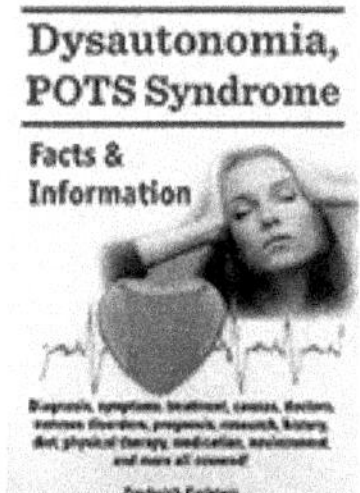

Dysautonomia, POTS Syndrome
Frederick Earlstein
978-0989658485

Degenerative Disc Disease Explained
Frederick Earlstein
978-0989658485

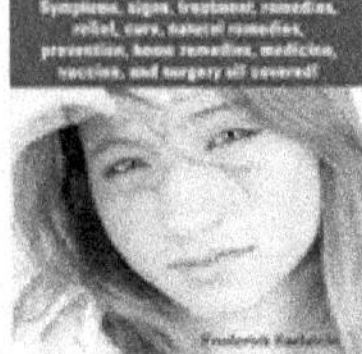

Sinusitis, Hay Fever,
Allergic Rhinitis Explained
Frederick Earlstein
978-1941070024

Wicca
Riley Star
978-1941070130

Zombie Apocalypse
Rex Cutty
978-1941070154

Capybara
Lolly Brown
978-1941070062

Eels As Pets
Lolly Brown
978-1941070167

Scabies and Lice Explained
Frederick Earlstein
978-1941070017

Saltwater Fish As Pets
Lolly Brown
978-0989658461

Torticollis Explained
Frederick Earlstein
978-1941070055

Kennel Cough
Lolly Brown
978-0989658409

Physiotherapist, Physical Therapist
Christopher Wright
978-0989658492

Rats, Mice, and Dormice As Pets
Lolly Brown
978-1941070079

Wallaby and Wallaroo Care
Lolly Brown
978-1941070031

Bodybuilding Supplements Explained
Jon Shelton
978-1941070239

Demonology
Riley Star
978-19401070314

Pigeon Racing
Lolly Brown
978-1941070307

Dwarf Hamster
Lolly Brown
978-1941070390

Cryptozoology
Rex Cutty
978-1941070406

Eye Strain
Frederick Earlstein
978-1941070369

Inez The Miniature Elephant
Asher Ray
978-1941070353

Vampire Apocalypse
Rex Cutty
978-1941070321

www.ingramcontent.com/pod-product-compliance
Lightning Source LLC
Chambersburg PA
CBHW052112090426
42741CB00009B/1773

* 9 7 8 1 9 4 6 2 8 6 5 3 6 *